MUSEUM ABC

THE METROPOLITAN MUSEUM OF ART
1000 Fifth Avenue, New York, NY 10028
www.metmuseum.org

Little, Brown and Company
Hachette Book Group
1290 Avenue of the Americas . New York, NY 10104
Visit our website at www.lb-kids.com

Little, Brown and Company is a division of Hachette Book Group, Inc.
The Little, Brown name and logo are trademarks of Hachette Book Group, Inc.

Little, Brown and Company is not responsible for websites (or their content)
that are not owned by Little, Brown and Company.

First Edition: September 2002

ISBN 978-0-316-07170-3 (Little, Brown and Company)
ISBN 978-1-58839-016-5 (MMA)
Library of Congress Control Number 2001096455

18

Printed in China

Produced by the Department of Special Publications, The Metropolitan Museum of Art:
Robie Rogge, Publishing Manager; Judith Cressy, Project Editor;
Christine Gardner, Editorial Assistant; Anna Raff, Designer; Victoria Gallina, Production Associate.
All photography by The Metropolitan Museum of Art Photograph Studio unless otherwise mentioned.

MUSEUM ABC

THE METROPOLITAN MUSEUM OF ART
New York

LITTLE, BROWN AND COMPANY
New York   Boston

is for APPLE.

B

is for BOAT.

is for CAT.

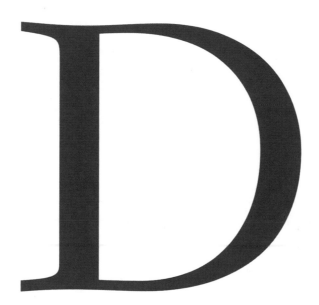

is for DANCE.

is for EGG.

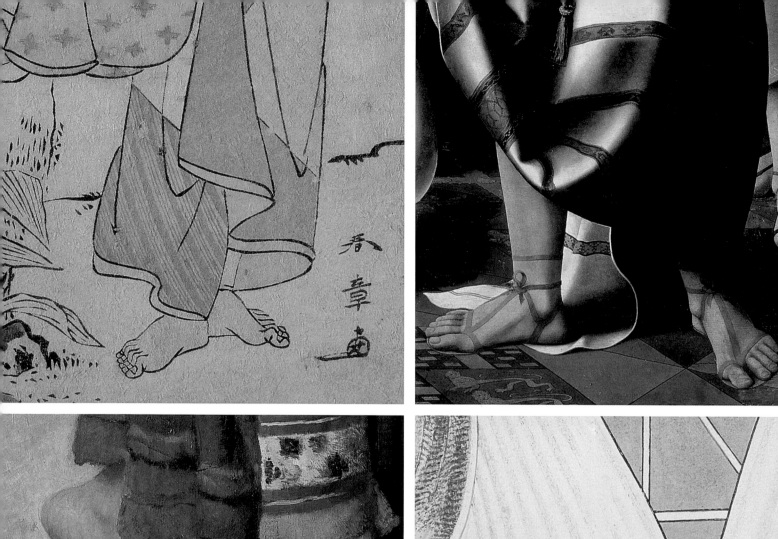
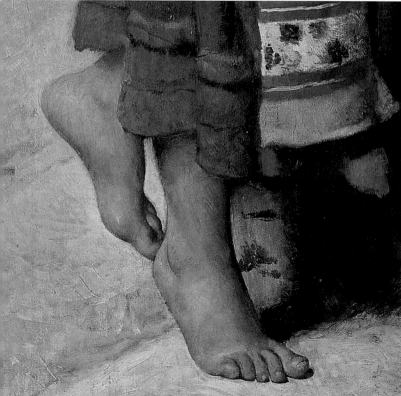

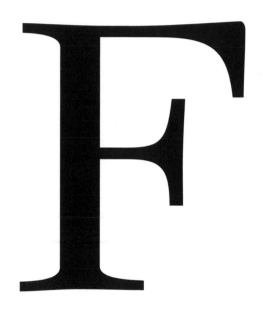

is for FEET.

is for GAME.

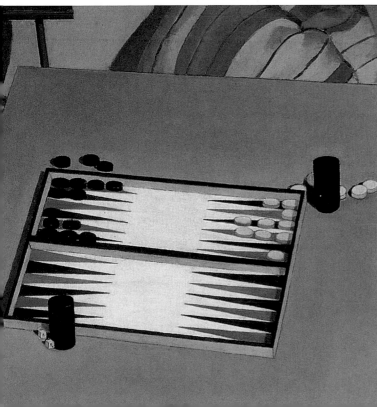

H

is for HAIR.

I

is for INSECT.

J

is for JEWELRY.

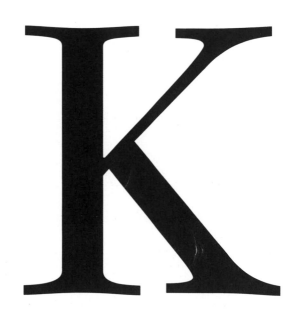

is for KISS.

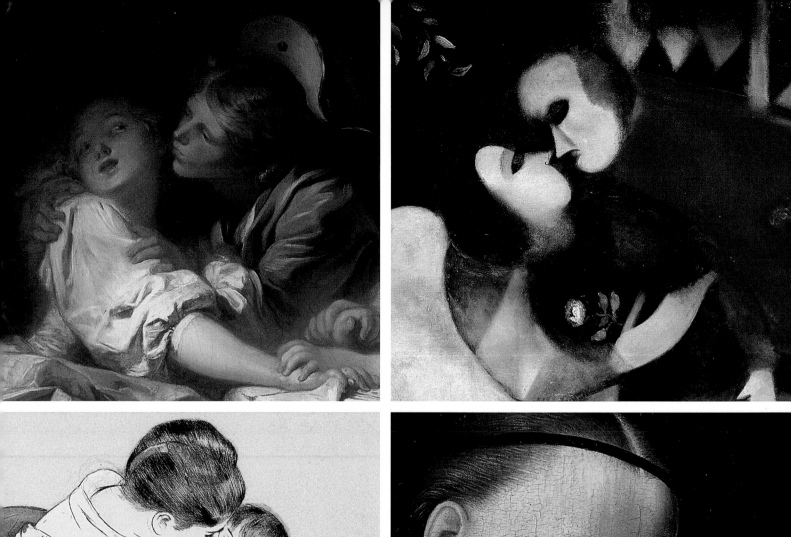

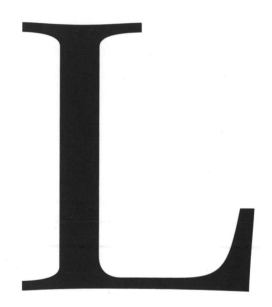

is for LIGHT.

M

is for MONSTER.

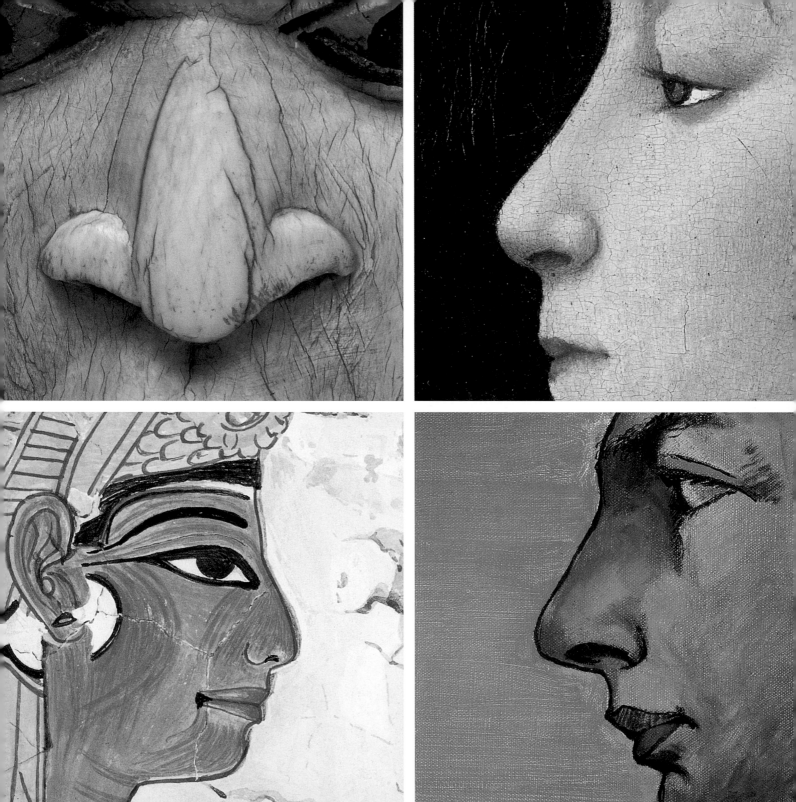

is for NOSE.

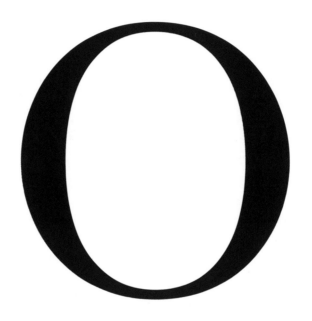

is for OX.

P

is for PEACOCK.

is for QUEEN.

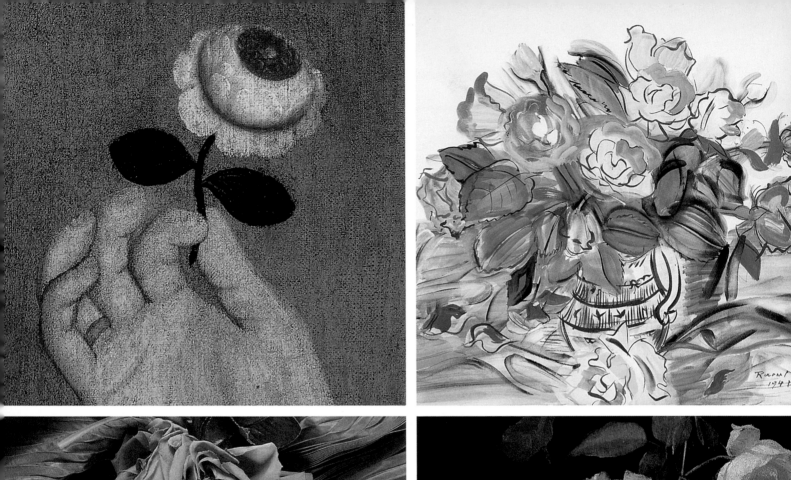

R

is for ROSE.

is for STAR.

is for TREE.

U
is for UMBRELLA.

is for VEGETABLE.

is for WINDOW.

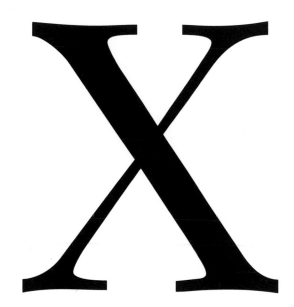

is for eX.

is for YELLOW.

is for ZIGZAG.

The captions correspond with the pictures on each page, reading clockwise from top left.

A

Red Apple (detail)
Roy Lichtenstein, American, 1923–1997
Woodcut, five-color, 30½ x 36 11/16 in., 1983
John B. Turner Fund, 1983 1983.1025

Apples (detail)
Paul Cézanne, French, 1839–1906
Oil on canvas, 9 x 13 in.
The Mr. and Mrs. Henry Ittleson Jr. Purchase Fund, 1961 61.103

Delicious Apples (detail)
Brian Connelly, American, 1926–1963
Watercolor on paper, 8¾ x 12¼ in., 1962
Gift of James Coats, in memory of the artist, 1966 66.227.1

Women Gathering Apples (detail)
Attributed to the Orchard Painter,
Greek, Attic, ca. 460 B.C.
Column-krater, terracotta, H. 17¾ in.
Rogers Fund, 1907 07.286.74

B

The Champion Single Sculls (Max Schmitt in a Single Scull) (detail)
Thomas Eakins, American, 1844–1916
Oil on canvas, 32¼ x 46¼ in., 1871
Purchase, The Alfred N. Punnett Endowment Fund and George D. Pratt Gift, 1934 34.92

Regatta at Sainte-Adresse (detail)
Claude Monet, French, 1840–1926
Oil on canvas, 29⅝ x 40 in.
Bequest of William Church Osborn, 1951 51.30.4

A Midnight Race on the Mississippi (detail)
Nathaniel Currier, American, 1813–1888, and
James Merritt Ives, American, 1824–1895, publishers
Hand-colored lithograph, 18 x 27¾ in., 1860
Bequest of Adele S. Colgate, 1962 63.550.5

Bamboo Yards at Kyobashi Bridge (detail)
Utagawa Hiroshige, Japanese, 1797–1858
Woodblock print in colors, from the series *One Hundred Famous Views of Edo*, 13⅞ x 9¼ in., 1857
Fletcher Fund, 1929 JP 1548

C

Caswell Carpet (detail)
Zeruah Higley Guernsey Caswell, American, 1805– ca. 1895
Colored woolen yarns embroidered on twill-weave woolen fabric, 13 ft. 4 in. x 12 ft. 3 in., ca. 1832–35
Gift of Katharine Keyes, in memory of her father, Homer Eaton Keyes, 1938 38.157

Little Grey Cat (detail)
Elizabeth Norton, American, 1887–1985
Printed color woodcut, 5⅛ x 4⅜ in.
Gift of Elizabeth Norton, 1928 28.63.1

Black Cat and Narcissus (detail)
Zhu Ling, Chinese, active about 1820–60
Qing dynasty
Hanging scroll, ink and color on paper, 36⅞ x 14½ in.
Rogers Fund, 1956 56.129.3

Joseph Interpreting the Dreams of His Fellow Prisoners (detail)
Master of the Story of Joseph, Netherlandish, ca. 1500
Oil on wood, Diam. 61½ in.
Harris Brisbane Dick Fund, 1953 53.168

D

Bugaku Dancers (detail)
Hanabusa Itchō, Japanese, 1652–1724
One of a pair of six-panel folding screens
Ink, color, and gold leaf on paper, 6 ft.⅛ in. x 14 ft. 9⅝ in., early 18th century
The Harry G. C. Packard Collection of Asian Art, Gift of Harry G. C. Packard, and Purchase, Fletcher, Rogers, Harris Brisbane Dick, and Louis V. Bell Funds, Joseph Pulitzer Bequest, and The Annenberg Fund Inc. Gift, 1975 1975.268.58

The Rehearsal Onstage (detail)
Edgar Degas, French, 1834–1917
Pastel over brush-and-ink drawing on paper, 21 x 28½ in.
H. O. Havemeyer Collection, Bequest of Mrs. H. O. Havemeyer, 1929 29.100.39

Dancing in Colombia (detail)
Fernando Botero, Colombian, b. 1932
Oil on canvas, 74 x 91 in., 1980
Anonymous Gift, 1983 1983.251

Dancing Dervishes (detail)
Indian, Mughal period, mid-16th century
From an album assembled for Emperor Shah Jahan
Colors and gold on paper, 15 5/16 x 10 9/16 in.
Rogers Fund and The Kevorkian Foundation Gift, 1955 55.121.10.18 r

E

Flowers by a Stone Vase (detail)
Peter Faes, Flemish, 1750–1814
Oil on wood, 20 x 14⅞ in.
Bequest of Catharine D. Wentworth, 1948 48.187.737

Brown and White Eggs (detail)
Brian Connelly, American, 1926–1963
Watercolor on paper, 8¾ x 12¼ in., 1962
Gift of James Coats, in memory of the artist, 1966 66.227.2

Leda and the Swan (detail)
Bacchiacca (Francesco d'Ubertino), Italian, Florentine, 1495–1557
Oil on wood, 16⅞ x 12½ in.
The Jack and Belle Linsky Collection, 1982 1982.60.11

The Broken Eggs (detail)
Jean Baptiste Greuze, French, 1725–1805
Oil on canvas, 28¾ x 37 in., 1756
Bequest of William K. Vanderbilt, 1920 20.155.8

F

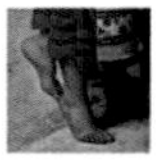

Ichikawa Danjūrō V (detail)
Katsukawa Shunshō, Japanese, 1726–1792
Polychrome woodblock print, 11⅝ x 5⅞ in., ca. 1773–74
Gift of Estate of Samuel Isham, 1914 JP 894

Moses and Aaron Before Pharaoh: An Allegory of the Dinteville Family (detail)
Master of the Dinteville Allegory, Netherlandish or French, active mid-16th century
Oil on wood, 69½ x 75⅞ in., 1537
Wentworth Fund, 1950 50.70

Ipuy and His Wife Receiving Offerings from Their Children (detail)
Egyptian, Thebes, Deir el Medina, 19th Dynasty
Copy of a wall painting from the Tomb of Ipuy, 18¼ x 29⅛ in., ca. 1275 B.C.
Rogers Fund, 1930 30.4.114

Roman Girl at a Fountain (detail)
Léon Bonnat, French, 1833–1922
Oil on canvas, 67 x 39½ in., 1875
Catharine Lorillard Wolfe Collection, Bequest of Catharine Lorillard Wolfe, 1887 87.15.137

G

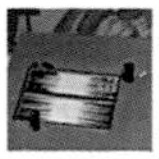

Boy with a House of Cards (detail)
François Hubert Drouais, French, 1727–1775
Oil on canvas, 28 x 23 in. (oval)
Gift of Mrs. William M. Haupt, from the collection of Mrs. James B. Haggin, 1965 65.242.1

Buzurjmihr Masters the Game of Chess (detail)
Firdausi, Iranian, Tabriz, ca. 1530–35
From the *Shah-nama* (*Book of Kings*), ink, silver, colors, and gold on paper, 9⅝ x 6⅞ in.
Gift of Arthur A. Houghton Jr., 1970 1970.301.71

Pool Parlor (detail)
Jacob Lawrence, American, 1917–2000
Gouache on paper, 31 x 22¾ in., 1942
Arthur Hoppock Hearn Fund, 1942 42.167

Americana (detail)
Charles Sheeler, American, 1883–1965
Oil on canvas, 48 x 36 in., 1931
Edith and Milton Lowenthal Collection, Bequest of Edith Abrahamson Lowenthal, 1991
1992.24.8

H

George Washington (detail)
Gilbert Stuart, American, 1755–1828
Oil on canvas, 30¼ x 25¼ in., 1795
Rogers Fund, 1907 07.160

Woman of the Pleasure District at Shinagawa (detail)
Kitagawa Utamaro, Japanese, 1753–1806
Polychrome woodblock print with mica ground, from the series *Beauties of the Southern District (Shinagawa)*, 14½ x $9\tfrac{5}{16}$ in., ca. 1793
Rogers Fund, 1922 JP 1367

Portrait of a Woman with a Dog (detail)
Jean Honoré Fragonard, French, 1732–1806
Oil on canvas, 32 x 25¾ in.
Fletcher Fund, 1937 37.118

Ipuy and His Wife Receiving Offerings from Their Children (detail)
Egyptian, Thebes, Deir el Medina, 19th Dynasty
Copy of a wall painting from the Tomb of Ipuy, 18¼ x 29⅛ in., ca. 1275 B.C.
Rogers Fund, 1930 30.4.114

I

Pink Roses with Wasps (detail)
Chinese, Qing dynasty
Handscroll, ink and color on silk, $9\tfrac{15}{16}$ x 79⅝ in.
From the Collection of A. W. Bahr, Purchase, Fletcher Fund, 1947 47.18.5

Study of Tulips (detail)
Jacob Marrel, Dutch, 1614–1681
Watercolor on vellum, $13\tfrac{3}{16}$ x $17\tfrac{15}{16}$ in.
Rogers Fund, 1968 68.66

Bees with Honeycomb (detail)
Candace Wheeler, American, 1827–1923
Wallpaper sheet, machine-printed colors and metallic colors on textured-weave paper, $9\tfrac{13}{16}$ x 20⅛ in., 1882
Gift of Sunworthy Wallcoverings, a Borden Company, 1987 1987.1074.1

Detail of a writing box
Japanese, 19th century
Sprinkled gold, inlay of shell and lead on black lacquer, 9¾ x 8 x 1⅛ in.
Bequest of Benjamin Altman, 1913 14.40.838 ab

J

Shah Jahan (detail)
Chitarman, Indian, Mughal period
From an album made for Emperor Shah Jahan, ink, opaque watercolor, and gold on paper, 15⅜ x 10⅛ in., 1627–28
Rogers Fund and The Kevorkian Foundation Gift, 1955 55.121.10.24

Francesco d'Este (detail)
Rogier van der Weyden, Netherlandish, 1399/1400–1464
Oil on wood, 12½ x 8¾ in., ca. 1460
The Friedsam Collection, Bequest of Michael Friedsam, 1931 32.100.43

Princesse de Broglie (detail)
Jean-Auguste-Dominique Ingres, French, 1780–1867
Oil on canvas, 47¾ x 35¾ in., 1851–53
Robert Lehman Collection, 1975 1975.1.186

Maria Portinari (Maria Maddlena Baroncelli) (detail)
Hans Memling, Netherlandish, active by 1465, d. by 1494
Oil on wood, 17⅜ x 13⅜ in.
Bequest of Benjamin Altman, 1913 14.40.627

K

The Stolen Kiss (detail)
Jean Honoré Fragonard, French, 1732–1806
Oil on canvas, 19 x 25 in.
Gift of Jessie Woolworth Donahue, 1956 56.100.1

The Lovers (detail)
Marc Chagall, French (b. Russia), 1887–1985
Oil on canvas, 43 x 53 in., 1913
Jacques and Natasha Gelman Collection, 1998
1999.363.14

Virgin and Child (detail)
Dieric Bouts, Netherlandish, active by 1457, d. 1475
Oil on wood, 8½ x 6½ in.
Theodore M. Davis Collection, Bequest of Theodore M. Davis, 1915 30.95.280

Mother's Kiss (detail)
Mary Cassatt, American, 1844–1926
Drypoint, aquatint, and soft-ground etching printed in color, 13⅝ x $8\tfrac{15}{16}$ in., ca. 1890–91
Gift of Paul J. Sachs, 1916 16.2.10

L

The Midnight Ride of Paul Revere (detail)
Grant Wood, American, 1892–1942
Oil on Masonite, 30 x 40 in., 1931
Arthur Hoppock Hearn Fund, 1950 50.117

Forging the Shaft (detail)
John Ferguson Weir, American, 1841–1926
Oil on canvas, 52 x 73¼ in., 1874–77
Purchase, Lyman G. Bloomingdale Gift, 1901 01.7.1

The Penitent Magdalen (detail)
Georges de La Tour, French, 1593–1652
Oil on canvas, 52½ x 40¼ in.
Gift of Mr. and Mrs. Charles Wrightsman, 1978
1978.517

Red Sunset on the Dnieper (detail)
Arkhip Ivanovich Kuindzhi, Russian, 1842–1910
Oil on canvas, 53 x 74 in.
Rogers Fund, 1974 1974.100

M

Ten Kings of Hell (detail)
Jin Chushi, Chinese, active late 12th century
Southern Song dynasty
One of a set of hanging scrolls, ink and color on silk, 44 x 18¾ in., before 1195
Rogers Fund, 1930 30.76.294
Photograph by Malcolm Varon

Fabulous Beast (detail)
Upper Rhenish, Basel, ca. 1420–30
Fragment of a tapestry hanging
Linen warp with wool weft, 28¾ x 33½ in.
The Cloisters Collection, 1990 1990.211

Illustrated Legends of the Kitano Tenjin Shrine (Kitano Tenjin Engi Emaki) (detail)
Japanese, Kamakura period, late 13th century
Handscroll, ink and color on paper, $11\frac{5}{16}$ x $8\frac{15}{16}$ in.
Fletcher Fund, 1925 25.224 d

Beauty and the Beast (detail)
Walter Crane, British, 1845–1915
Book illustration
Reissue, *Walter Crane's Picture Books*, large series, engraved and printed by Edmund Evans for John Lane, London and New York
The Elisha Whittelsey Collection, The Elisha Whittelsey Fund, 1972 1972.655.1

N

Detail of a pendant mask
African, Nigeria, Court of Benin, 16th century
Ivory, iron, and copper, H. 9⅜ in.
The Michael C. Rockefeller Memorial Collection, Gift of Nelson A. Rockefeller, 1972 1978.412.323

Portrait of a Woman (detail)
Master of the Castello Nativity, Italian, Florentine, active ca. 1445–75
Tempera and gold on canvas, 15¾ x 10¾ in.
The Jules Bache Collection, 1949 49.7.6

Self-Portrait (detail)
Giorgio de Chirico, Italian (b. Greece), 1888–1978
Oil on canvas, 34⅜ x 27½ in., 1911
Gift in memory of Carl Van Vechten and Fania Marinoff, 1970 1970.166

Nefertari Kneeling in Adoration (detail)
Egyptian, Thebes, Valley of the Queens, 19th Dynasty
Copy of a wall painting from the tomb of Nefertari, 18⅛ x 13⅜ in., 1279–1213 B.C.
Rogers Fund, 1930 30.4.144

O

Detail of a plaque from a book cover
South Italian, perhaps Benevento, ca. 975–1000
Ivory, 9¼ x 5⅜ in.
Gift of J. Pierpont Morgan, 1917 17.190.38

Ox Team, Matinicus (detail)
George Bellows, American, 1882–1925
Oil on wood, 22 x 28 in., 1916
Gift of Mr. and Mrs. Raymond J. Horowitz, 1974 1974.352

Estate Activities (detail)
Egyptian, Thebes, 18th Dynasty
Copy of a wall painting from the tomb of Nakht, 89 x 66½ in., ca. 1400 B.C.
Rogers Fund, 1915 15.5.19 b

The Adoration of the Magi (detail)
Style of Hieronymus Bosch, Netherlandish, ca. 1550
Oil and gold on wood, 28 x 22¼ in.
John Stewart Kennedy Fund, 1913 13.26

P

Madonna and Child with Saints (detail)
Girolamo dai Libri, Italian, Veronese, 1474–1555
Tempera and oil on canvas, 13 ft. 1 in. x 6 ft. 9½ in.
Fletcher Fund, 1920 20.92

Peacock (detail)
Probably after a design by Tiffany Studios, American, ca. 1913
Wool and silk on linen, 72 x 32¾ in.
Gift of Edgar Kaufmann Jr., 1969 69.260

Krishna Fluting (detail)
Indian, Rajasthan, probably Amber, ca. 1610
Page from the *Rasikapriya* (*Garden of Delights*), ink and opaque watercolor on paper, 9 x 5⅝ in.
Rogers Fund, 1918 18.85.5a

The Modern Poster (detail)
Will H. Bradley, American, 1868–1962
Commercial lithograph, Charles Scribner's Sons, New York, $19\frac{13}{16}$ x 12⅞ in., 1895
Purchase, Leonard A. Lauder Gift, 1990 1990.1016.1

Q

Reine (detail)
Lucien La Forge, French, b. ca. 1885, d. ?
Woodcut, printed in colors, from an alphabet book published by Henry Goulet, Paris, 20th century
Harris Brisbane Dick Fund, 1930 30.96.7

The Execution of Saint John the Baptist and the Presentation of the Baptist's Head to Herod (detail)
Master of the Life of Saint John the Baptist, Italian, Romagnole, active first third 14th century
Tempera on wood, gold ground, 17⅜ x 19⅝ in.
Robert Lehman Collection, 1975 1975.1.103

Two Riddles of the Queen of Sheba (detail)
Upper Rhenish, Strasbourg, 1490–1500
Bast fiber warp, wool, silk, and metallic wefts; wool pile yarns, 31½ x 40 in.
The Cloisters Collection, 1971 1971.43

Queen Victoria (detail)
Thomas Sully, American, 1783–1872
Oil on canvas, 36 x 28⅜ in., 1838
Bequest of Francis T. Sully Darley, 1914 14.126.1

R

Young Lady with a Rose (detail)
Attributed to Pieter Vanderlyn, American, ca. 1687–1778
Oil on canvas, 32½ x 27 in., 1732
Gift of Edgar William and Bernice Chrysler Garbisch, 1962 62.256.1

Roses in a Blue Bowl (detail)
Raoul Dufy, French, 1877–1953
Watercolor on paper, $27\frac{11}{16}$ x 33¼, 1941
Bequest of Loula D. Lasker, New York City, 1961 61.145.1

Roses (detail)
George Cochran Lambdin, American, 1830–1896
Oil on wood, 24 x 11⅞ in., 1878
Gift of Mrs. Manfred P. Welcher, 1918 18.116

Detail of a ball gown
Cristobal Balenciaga, French (b. Spain), 1895–1972
Pleated pink taffeta with matching pink silk roses, winter 1947–48
Given by Lisa and Jody Greene, in memory of their loving mother, Ethel S. Greene, 1958 CI.58.13.6 ab

S

The Nativity (detail)
German, Boppard-on-the-Rhine, Carmelite Church of Unserer Lieben Frau, ca. 1440–46
Pot metal, white glass, vitreous paint, silver stain, and olive-green enamel, 43¼ x 29¼ in.
Francis L. Leland Fund, 1913 13.64.4

Landscape with Stars (detail)
Henri-Edmond Cross, French, 1856–1910
Watercolor and graphite on paper, 9⅝ x 12¾ in.
Robert Lehman Collection, 1975 1975.1.592

Detail from a basin
Iranian, early 14th century
Brass, inlaid with silver and gold, H. 5⅛ in., Diam. 20½ in.
Edward C. Moore Collection, Bequest of Edward C. Moore, 1891 91.1.521

Detail from a set design for *The Magic Flute*
Karl Friedrich Schinkel, German, 1781–1841
Hand- and plate-colored aquatint, 11¼ x 14¾ in., 1819
The Elisha Whittelsey Collection, The Elisha Whittelsey Fund, 1954 54.602.1 (14)

T

The Four Trees (detail)
Claude Monet, French, 1840–1926
Oil on canvas, 32¼ x 32⅛ in., 1891
H. O. Havemeyer Collection, Bequest of Mrs. H. O. Havemeyer, 1929 29.100.110

The Lightning That Struck Rufo Barcliff (detail)
Carroll Cloar, American, 1913–1993
Tempera on composition board, 31 x 23 in., 1955
George A. Hearn Fund, 1956 56.40

Detail from a Nō robe
Japanese, Edo period, 19th century
Silk and gold brocade, L. 59⅜ in.
Gift of Mrs. Russell Sage, by exchange, 1979
1979.408

Afternoon Among the Cypress (detail)
Arthur Frank Mathews, American, 1860–1945
Oil on canvas, 26¼ x 30 in.
Gift of Mrs. Henrietta Zeile, 1909 09.186

U

The Little Laundry Girl (La Petite Blanchisseuse) (detail)
Pierre Bonnard, French, 1867–1947
Lithograph printed in five colors, 11¾ x 7½ in. 1895–96
Harris Brisbane Dick Fund, 1939 39.102.3

Buttercups (detail)
Daniel Kelly, American, b. 1947
Woodblock print, 9½ x 30 in., 1983
Anonymous Gift, 1986 JP 3698

Shower at the New Yanagi Bridge with Rainbow at Mitakegura (detail)
Katsushika Hokusai, Japanese, 1760–1849
Polychrome woodblock print, 7⅞ x 11¾ in., 1806
The Howard Mansfield Collection, Purchase, Rogers Fund, 1936 JP 2580

At the Seaside (detail)
William Merritt Chase, American, 1849–1916
Oil on canvas, 20 x 34 in., ca. 1892
Bequest of Miss Adelaide Milton de Groot (1876–1967), 1967 67.187.123

V

Onions and Tomato (detail)
Mary Ann Currier, American, b. 1927
Oil pastel on matboard, 26½ x 56 in.
Purchase, Dr. and Mrs. Robert E. Carroll Gift, 1985
1985.78

Still Life with Strawberries (detail)
French, 17th century
Oil on canvas, 23⅜ x 31⅝ in.
Bequest of Harry G. Sperling, 1971 1976.100.10

Red Cabbage, Rhubarb, and Orange (detail)
Charles Demuth, American, 1883–1935
Watercolor on paper, 14 x 19⅞ in.
Alfred Stieglitz Collection, 1949 49.70.57

Still Life: Balsam Apple and Vegetables (detail)
James Peale, American, 1749–1831
Oil on canvas, 20¼ x 26½ in., ca. 1820s
Maria DeWitt Jesup Fund, 1939 39.52

W

Girl at a Window (detail)
Balthus, French, 1908–2001
Oil on canvas, 63 x 63¾ in., 1957
Jacques and Natasha Gelman Collection, 1998
1999.363.3
Photograph by Malcolm Varon

The Annunciation Triptych (detail from central panel)
Robert Campin and assistant (possibly Rogier van der Weyden), Flemish, ca. 1425–30
Oil on wood, central panel 25¼ x 24⅞ in.
The Cloisters Collection, 1956 56.70

Thursday (detail)
John Moore, American, b. 1941
Oil on canvas, 92 x 141 in., 1980
George A. Hearn Fund, 1983 1983.170

Ricefields in Asakusa on the Day of the Torinomachi Festival (detail)
Utagawa Hiroshige, Japanese, 1797–1858
Polychrome woodblock print from the series *One Hundred Famous Views of Edo*, 13 1/16 x 8 11/16 in., 1857
Rogers Fund, 1914 JP 60

X

Crisscrossed Conveyors, River Rouge Plant, Ford Motor Company (detail)
Charles Sheeler, American, 1883–1965
Gelatin silver print, 9 5/16 x 7 7/16 in., 1927
Ford Motor Company Collection, Gift of Ford Motor Company and John C. Waddell, 1987 1987.1100.1

Haines City
Frank Stella, American, b. 1936
Acrylic on canvas, 99 x 99 in., 1963
Gift of Stanley Crantson, 1988 1988.223

January (detail)
Franz M. Melchers, Belgian, 1868–1944
Handtinted lithograph illustration from *L'An* (poems by Thomas Braun), published by E. Lyon-Claesen, Brussels, 9 15/16 x 9 15/16 in., 1897
The Elisha Whittelsey Collection, The Elisha Whittelsey Fund, 1967 67.763.1

Detail of a leper mask
African, Burkina Faso, Bwa peoples, 20th century
Wood and pigment, 34¾ x 9¾ in.
Gift of Thomas G. B. Wheelock, 1997 1997.444.7

Y

City and Sunset (detail)
Henry Farrer, American, 1843–1903
Watercolor on off-white wove paper, 9⅟₁₆ x 11⅝₁₆ in.
Purchase, Gifts of Mrs. Louis Lamson and Mrs. Alfred
N. Lawrence, Bequest of Antoinette D. T.
Throckmorton, in memory of Jules and Ella Turcas,
and Bequest of May Blackstone Huntington, by
exchange; Mr. and Mrs. Harry L. Koenigsberg, Walter
Knight Sturges and Vain and Harry Fish Foundation
Gifts, and Maria Dewitt Jesup Fund, 1985   1985.107.2

The Port at Saint-Tropez (detail)
Paul Signac, French, 1863–1935
Color lithograph in seven colors, trial proof, 17⅛ x 13
in., 1898
The Elisha Whittelsey Collection, The Elisha
Whittelsey Fund, 1987   1987.1087

Boy with Baseball (detail)
George Luks, American, 1866–1933
Oil on canvas, 30 x 25 in., ca. 1925
The Edward Joseph Gallagher III Memorial
Collection, Gift of Edward Joseph Gallagher Jr., 1954
54.10.2

Autumn River (detail)
Wolf Kahn, American, b. 1927
Oil on canvas, 52 x 72 in., 1979
Purchase, The Martin S. Ackerman Foundation Gift,
1979   1979.184

Z

Detail of an apron
African, Cameroon, 19th–20th century
Fiber, glass beads, cowrie shells, 13 x 14¾ in.
Gift of Cecilia and Irwin Smiley, 1979   1979.532.14

Detail of a ceiling pattern
Egyptian, Thebes, 18th Dynasty
Copy of a painting from the tomb of Nakht,
50 x 55⅛ in., ca. 1400 B.C.
Rogers Fund, 1915   15.5.19 h

*Yatsushashi (The Bridge of Eight Parts) in
Mikawa* (detail)
Katsushika Hokusai, Japanese, 1760–1849
Polychrome woodblock print, 9⅛ x 14⅝ in., 1827–30
Rogers Fund, 1922   JP 1398

After Sir Christopher Wren (detail)
Charles Demuth, American, 1883–1935
Watercolor, gouache, and pencil on cardboard, 24 x 20
in., 1920
Bequest of Scofield Thayer, 1982   1984.433.156

ABCDE
MNOPQ
WXYZA
HIJKLM